Tony's SUPERHERO Story

Written by
**Anthony "Tony"
Santilli, LMFT**

Illustrated by
**Monique
Belmedioni**

To order additional copies of this book, contact:
Xlibris
844-714-8691
www.Xlibris.com
Orders@Xlibris.com

ISBN: 978-1-6641-1059-5 (sc)
ISBN: 978-1-6641-1060-1 (hc)
ISBN: 978-1-6641-1058-8 (e)

Library of Congress Control Number: 2021920759

Print information available on the last page

Rev. date: 10/20/2021

DEDICATION

Tony's Superhero Story is dedicated to the sixteen-year-old Tony Santilli, who attempted suicide by drowning. This book honors everyone who has suffered the pain and misery of suicide ideation, lost a loved one to suicide, and struggled with their mental health and/or identity.

Tony's Superhero Story is influenced by psychology and the wellness books *Superhero Therapy* by Janina Scarlet and *The Wild Unknown Animal Spirit* by Kim Krans. I drew inspiration from my favorite fantasy stories, animated shows, musicians, songs, and movies.

BACKSTORY

Tony's Superhero Story was first written in early 2021 when Tony was preparing to study for his clinical licensure exam to become a licensed Marriage and Family Therapist. He experienced nervousness in anticipation of this 170-question exam and felt anxious due to the coronavirus pandemic. To help reduce these negative emotions, Tony began to write his life story. During the writing process, Tony decided to change his context to the superhero and fantasy genres, which he has enjoyed since early childhood. The water aspect came naturally to Tony, who has always been drawn to water since birth. After titling the parts of *Tony's Superhero Story* and finishing the first draft, Tony felt in control of his anxiety and realized that this written self-healing story could be a book to benefit everyone. Before passing his licensure exam, Tony began to develop his story into a book by consulting with the editors, hiring Monique to create the artwork, and hiring John for his expertise.

ACKNOWLEDGMENTS

Thank you, Tony's Superhero Squad!

Thank you to the editors (the Slytherin trio) of *Tony's Superhero Story*: Annie Jung, Kevin Fuquay, and Lauren Weber. Your guidance and inspiration sparked the magic of this book. Without your insights and recommendations, this book would not exist.

Thank you to John Castle for your web design, social media advice, and assistance with publishing *Tony's Superhero Story*. I appreciate your passion and motivation to make the book come alive.

My sincerest gratitude to Monique Belmedioni for your fantastically detailed illustrations. I am thankful for your flexibility during the five months of work on this project and for your creative ideas to improve the original sketches.

A huge thank you to the group of friends who contributed to the Suicide Prevention and Awareness Month commencement post: Nick Karkas (photographer), Jessica Achermann (artistic director), and Aaron Petty and Federico Aramburu (emotional support squad).

Thank you to my lifelong friend, Kevin Gaan, for being the first friend I shared the idea of this book with and for your full support throughout my journey as a first-time author.

Most importantly, thank you to my mom, dad, and sister for your endless support in my writing and life journeys. I love you all so much.

CONTENTS

A Boy Who Loves Water

PART 1

Not too long ago, a boy named Tony was born and raised in a seaside village called Belmont, known to honor a magical place in the ocean called the Water Kingdom. No one from Belmont had ever seen the Water Kingdom due to it being deep underwater, but Tony had heard amazing legends about the beauty and serenity of the Water Kingdom from family and village folks. The stories told of a place where dolphins and other animals lived in peace and tranquility in loving and thriving communities called pods. Whenever Tony watched dolphins swim above the water, he fantasized about visiting the Water Kingdom with the dolphins.

The dolphins enjoyed watching Tony swim and also observed and admired his kindness toward everyone. Even though there was no verbal communication between Tony and the dolphins, the dolphins decided to teach Tony a Water Kingdom martial art called waterbending. Waterbending is based on the four swimming strokes, and each stroke has a main technique created by different water animals to control and bend the element of water: butterfly (dolphins), backstroke (otters), breaststroke (frogs), and freestyle (sharks). These animals each have different waterbending cultures: dolphins are social and receptive, otters are playful and adventurous, frogs are adaptable and calming, and sharks are bold and straightforward. For years, Tony enjoyed his butterfly lessons from the dolphins. Tony used his butterfly technique to play with the dolphins in the majestic blue ocean and taught butterfly to younger kids from Belmont. Tony perceived the dolphins' happiness living in the Water Kingdom and hoped to one day use his butterfly waterbending skills to visit it and swim with the dolphins.

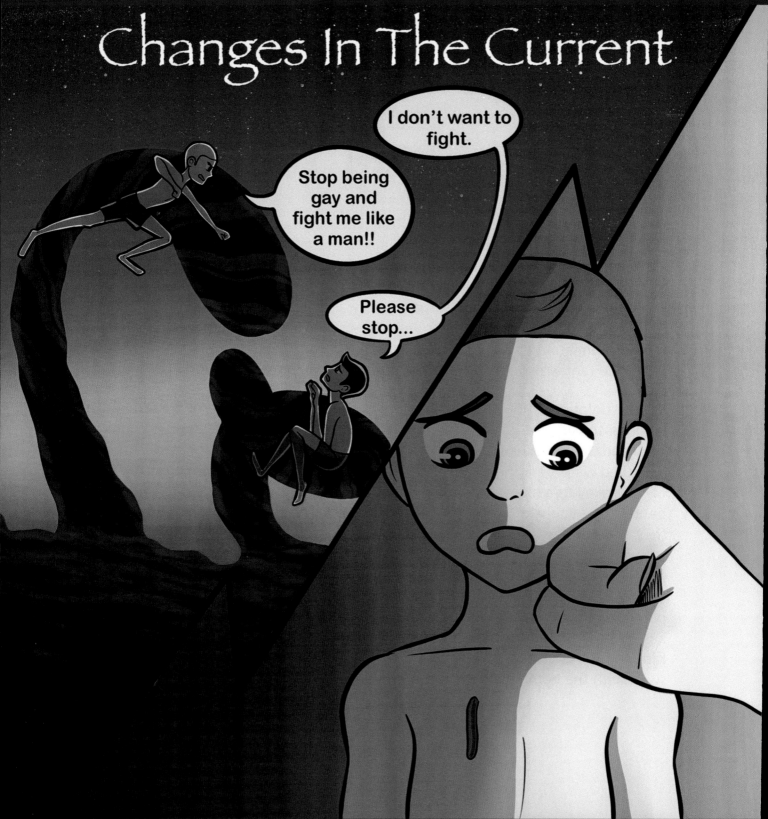

PART 2

As Tony entered his teen years, he began to feel uncomfortable with his body. He experienced a phase when he had to wear glasses to see properly and felt self-conscious about his appearance. Although Tony remained social and receptive to others, he didn't feel understood. The ocean water became slightly darker, but he was still enthused about dolphins and the Water Kingdom. Tony also began to acknowledge that he liked boys but felt confused by this part of his identity.

In his mid-teens, he was part of a competitive waterbending team that featured a waterbender from each of the four animal styles. The team's freestyle (shark) waterbender, Brian, did not like that Tony's waterbending was the strength of the team. He felt envious of Tony's butterfly and, for months, persistently called Tony a fag. Tony struggled to stand up for himself; Brian humiliated and degraded Tony by claiming dolphins aren't manly, pantsing his swimming trunks, and shaming his identity. The dolphins did everything they could to protect Tony, but Brian's shark friends used aggressive gestures to intimidate the dolphins.

During a competition, Tony felt the bullying was too much and pleaded for Brian to stop. Instead, Brian used different freestyle moves to attack him. Tony used his butterfly to protect himself, but Brian hurled derogatory phrases to overwhelm him. Tony was terrified as the dolphins became scared and fled the scene for their safety. The sharks chased after the dolphins, leaving Tony and Brian alone. Brian launched an aggressive freestyle attack. Tony attempted to use butterfly, but Brian foresaw the move and escalated his behavior to physically assaulting Tony. Following the assault, Brian took advantage of his own bloody nose to smear his blood all across Tony's chest, while insultingly calling him gay. The ocean color became significantly darker.

Drowning

PART 3

Tony was devastated after Brian used shark attacks on him, feeling both humiliated and emasculated. Tony knew that he liked boys and dolphins but believed that they were the source of his pain. He wanted the pain to stop, but it only increased with time. Tony couldn't ignore his suffering and wanted to be like the boy who loves water. Over the next year, Tony searched the surfaces of the dark ocean for the dolphins, but they had disappeared. He felt abandoned and unsure of why he couldn't see them. Tony didn't have the coping skills to take care of himself and was frightened to embrace his identity and vulnerability, preferring to deny these qualities. Tony's mind often replayed the traumatic bullying event. He was struggling to accept himself and despaired at the dolphins' absence. Without them, Tony became depressed and lonely.

He thought no one would understand or care about his hardships. He attempted to reach out for help, but most boys told him to simply "man up." Discouraged and fearing judgment, Tony was too frightened to reach out further. He didn't know of any superheroes he could relate to because they all seemed either so confident in their identity, or none of the men identified as LGBTQIA+. Tony tried for a while to deny his depression, but his well-being continued to sink. At this time, Tony felt completely empty, and he felt no control in his life. He experienced growing motivation to end his life because he believed that killing himself was the only way to end his misery.

One night, Tony swam out into the dark-blue-and-purple ocean until he could no longer see Belmont. Tony used his butterfly technique to surround himself with water, hoping to never come up for air again. He felt numb and gradually struggled to stay underwater. He needed air but fought the urge to breathe. Thinking he hated himself and believing he could never be happy again, Tony was determined to end his suffering. Feelings began to numb, thoughts became fuzzy, and his body felt light. The water was nearly black. The end was in sight.

Globally, suicide is the second-highest cause of death for people aged fifteen to twenty-four years old. Suicide is the tenth leading cause of death in the USA for all ages. LGBTQIA+ youth are almost five times more likely to attempt suicide compared to heterosexual youth. No matter the story, suicide is a tragic, painful, and heartbreaking way of dying. There are ways to prevent deaths by suicide and deaths by drowning. For more information, visit the following:

- The Trevor Project
- Save Suicide Awareness Voices of Education
- Newport Academy
- The Michael Phelps Foundation

Water Reflections

PART 4

Tony was now deathly still, deep under the water's surface, and only a few bubbles escaped his mouth. Just at the brink of fully drowning, there was a sudden, powerful unconscious sensation for Tony to save himself—he used what little strength he had left to swim up to the surface. He gasped for air, breathing heavily as he gained more awareness and realized how close to death he had been. Tony swam out of the dark ocean and ran onto the beach, running until he stumbled upon a nearby creek. At the creek, there was a shell phone labeled Superhero Lifeline. Tony called and spoke to a thoughtful superhero who helped him by using a breaststroke (frog) waterbending technique to play soothing frog and water noises.

After listening to these sounds and taking a few deep breaths, Tony ended the phone call. He saw his sad reflection in the creek and shed a tear. He did not want to see water or himself. He tried over and over to use his butterfly technique to bend the water away, but the water no longer moved. The creek water continued to shine with Tony's reflection. He stared at the creek in shock that he could no longer waterbend and grieved with an increasing sense of shame over his drowning attempt. He slapped the water and cried, "Who am I? What's the point of my existence?" These questions deepened his depression and caused his self-esteem to sink.

Speaking to a waterbender on the Superhero Lifeline prompted Tony to ponder what a superhero means to him. In Tony's view, he saw a superhero as someone who helps anyone who is suffering and is able to support themselves simultaneously. Tony's heart dropped when he had this thought because he felt the polar opposite from a superhero. He didn't have any powers after losing his waterbending and had no strength to help anyone. Tony couldn't even take care of himself or trust his own decision-making. He didn't understand his identity and felt unworthy to be a superhero. These thoughts terrified him every time he was at the ocean or when he saw his reflection.

For the next several months, to avoid his problems, Tony did not visit the ocean or look at himself in the mirror. His heart overflowed with feelings of guilt and disgust toward himself. Tony's parents urged him to see a Magical Healer in Belmont. He felt ambivalent about seeing the Magical Healer but went anyway because he felt hopelessly shattered.

PART 5

The Magical Healer introduced himself and described the Superhero Recovery process, which is when any superhero going through a challenging time needs a private space to heal, grow, and learn. Since Tony radiated a magical aura, the Magical Healer believed that he and Tony would get along well. After receiving Tony's permission, he proceeded to use a spell to playfully levitate Tony with gentle, dancing rainbow winds. This magical experience exhilarated Tony, who had thought that magic only existed in the Water Kingdom. The Magical Healer said Tony would learn about magic later but that Tony's well-being was the true priority.

Tony built up the courage to talk about the traumas he had with water. The magic helped Tony explore his feelings and process his experiences. Tony often cried, but the Magical Healer trained him to handle his emotions like a superhero, mentoring him in the areas of self-compassion and compassion for others and leading him to peaceful acceptance of his identity. Believing in Tony's potential and strength, the Magical Healer instilled hope in him that he would one day see the dolphins again and visit the Water Kingdom. His encouragement perplexed Tony; he had never received support like this before but noticed improvements with his well-being and mental health.

Tony went through the Superhero Recovery process for six months. As time passed, the supportive Magical Healer recommended that Tony return to the ocean. Tony had doubts because he had not returned to the ocean since his suicide attempt, but his dedication to self-love and confidence proved stronger. He went to the ocean. On the beach, Tony nervously attempted his butterfly technique several times and failed every time. The water didn't move, but Tony recalled how much progress he had made in his superhero journey and focused his powers. Suddenly, *bam!* A blue spark ignited from his finger!

The light invigorated Tony. Tony had unlocked a spell within himself called water magic: healing. When he returned to the Magical Healer to tell him of this accomplishment, the Magical Healer explained that magic is accessible to everyone but that superheroes who are motivated to be their authentic, best selves could naturally acquire spells. Tony learned there are three ways to acquire spells: hard work and commitment, perseverance in the face of a life-threatening crisis, and innate intuition. He had thought his water magic was not manly, but the Magical Healer reminded Tony of his tremendous growth. This encouragement inspired an exhilarating sense of hope, so Tony began using his water magic.

Becoming A Water Curer

 **Air**

- BREATHING TECHNIQUES
- DANCE
- MUSIC
- PERSPECTIVE SHIFTS

 **Fire**

- ARTS AND CRAFTS
- BAKING
- RECONNECT TO YOUR "INNER FIRE"
- TRATAKA

 **Earth**

- GROUNDING TECHNIQUES
- HIKING
- NATURE
- STRENGTH TRAINING

 **Water**

- BODIES OF WATER
- DRINKING H2O
- SHOWERS AND BATHS
- SWIMMING

Healing

- EATING MINDFULLY
- FACE MASKS
- REGULAR SELF-CARE
- REST

 **Magic**

- ADVENTURES/ TRAVEL
- ANIMALS
- FRIENDS
- READING

Spirit

- LEARNING
- MEDITATION
- STEP INTO THE UNKNOWN
- TALK THERAPY

PART 6

Tony used his newfound powers throughout the village of Belmont and grew interested in helping others begin their own superhero journeys. All superheroes have, at some point, felt powerlessness, despair, or suffering, but a superhero is someone who is brave and honest about those vulnerabilities and wants to lift up other superheroes. Tony realized that he never wanted anyone to feel suicidal or in pain. This epiphany sparked his motivation to use his healing for the benefit of all superheroes. Tony completed his time with the Magical Healer with a solidified sense of purpose to use his water magic: healing spell. The Magical Healer wished Tony the best on his spiritual journey as they parted ways.

When he turned eighteen years old, Tony began to study at the Elemental Hero Academy. Each year, he studied the four elements on our planet: air, fire, earth, and water. Tony wanted to understand how the other lands used their element to heal and be magical and traveled to seek further wisdom.

Himali Hawa (Mount Air)
La Isla del Fuego (Fire Island)
Provincia della Terra (Earth Province)
The Dam Falls (Waterfalls)

Tony embraced the various cultures, superheroes, healing, and the magic of each element. He learned healing strategies from superheroes in each culture on how they cured other superheroes in crises: air is about moving decisively with freedom, fire is about going through the fiery discomfort to transform, earth is about our instinct to survive and ground ourselves, and water is about our ability to emotionally express ourselves. Tony greatly enjoyed his adventures abroad and appreciated that each element contributed to his magical growth to heal others. Four years of travel inspired Tony to aspire to become a Magical Healer.

Remembering the Magical Healer's departing words, *spiritual journey*, Tony thought deeply about what *spirit* meant. He reflected on spiritual moments when he had been notably challenged, had an awakening with his soul, or was at a crossroad in his life. He had learned that a spiritual journey is about embracing the unknown and accepting the flow of life with all its bends, changes, and joys. His spiritual journey had led him to pursue happiness and fulfillment, yet he couldn't forget about and missed the dolphins from the Water Kingdom. Just as he had done as a small child, he once again fantasized about the Water Kingdom and how meaningful it would be to visit it in person. Although Tony didn't realize it, the dolphins had been missing him too.

Becoming A Water Curer

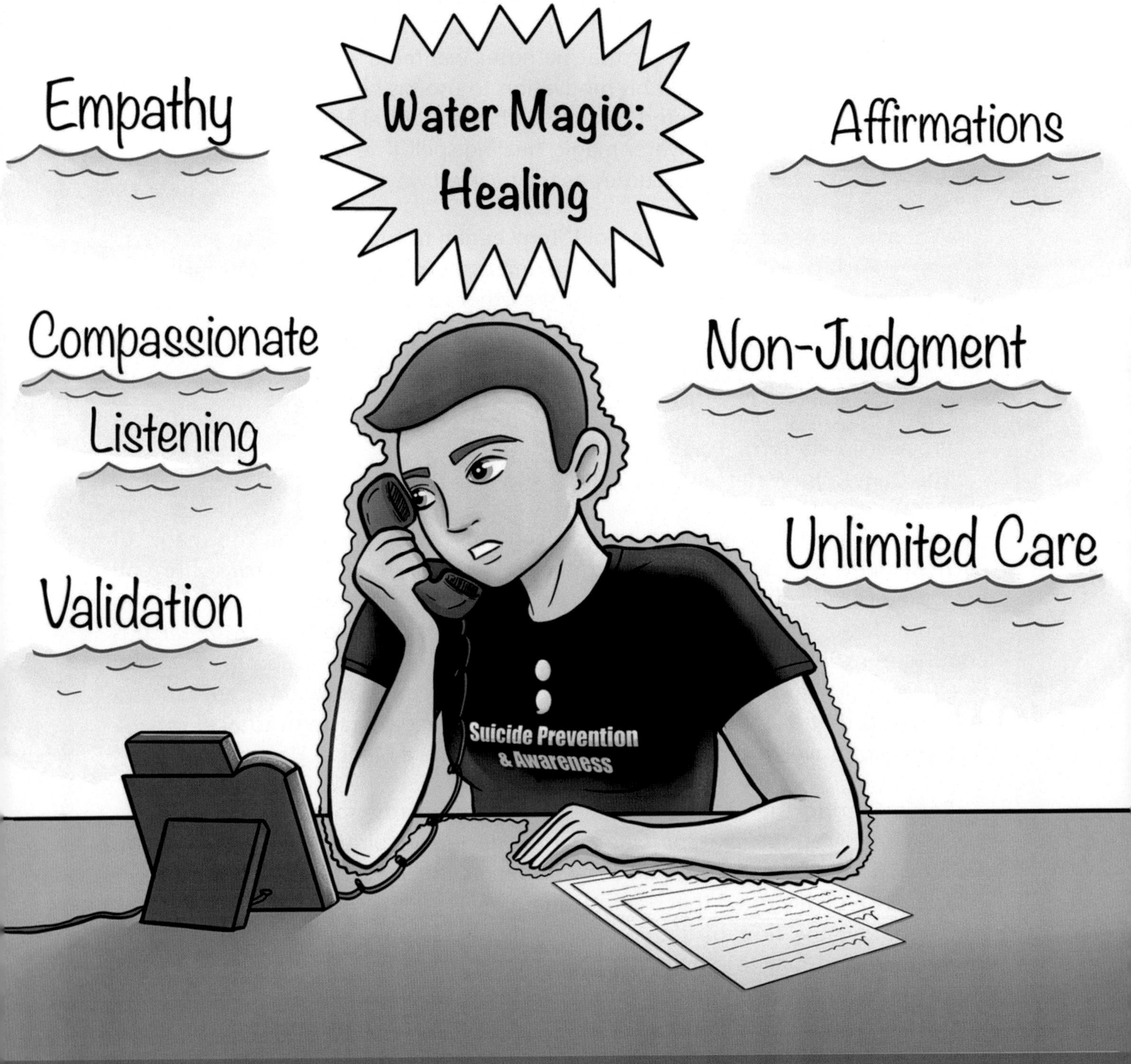

PART 6

After graduating from the Elemental Hero Academy, Tony wanted to continue developing his water magic: healing spell and become an official Magical Healer. He was thrilled when he was chosen to study at the Sorcery Institute for Healing. Throughout the three years at this advanced program, Tony studied and practiced how to apply his water magic: healing spell to superheroes in Superhero Recovery. He learned how to embrace and maximize the six core components of this powerful spell: empathy, affirmations, compassionate listening, non-judgment, validation, and unlimited care. The magic that had once only lived in the tip of his finger transformed and now flowed through Tony's entire being. When he became a professional Magical Healer, he had the traditional option to call himself a Magical Healer or create his own title. Tony decided to incorporate his water background and called himself the Water Curer.

As a professional Water Curer, Tony confidently used his magic to help stabilize and support superheroes who felt suicidal or were in crisis. He decided to volunteer at the very same Superhero Lifeline that had once saved his life. The water magic: healing allowed Tony to heal superheroes from different lands, and he listened to thousands of hardships. Tony felt passionate about his mission and felt fulfilled by helping superheroes who wanted to heal and grow. Sometimes, a superhero described a hardship similar to the one he had faced, and the memory of drowning made Tony feel uneasy, but with his wisdom, he guided both himself and the suffering superhero to a better and safer emotional place.

Tony incorporated healing strategies from across the four elements, tailoring his lessons to each superhero's strengths and culture. He never gave up on anyone, no matter who they were. Any superhero who shared parts of their spirit and vulnerabilities was courageous and showed their determination to grow into a stronger superhero. He always felt humbled that superheroes trusted his Water Curer superhero identity. The more Tony heard of others' spirits, the more he reflected on his own spirit.

Tony loved his magical healing capabilities, but he missed freely swimming in the ocean with the dolphins. Years had passed, and Tony wondered how the ocean near Belmont was faring. Tony believed his magic could be enough to find the Water Kingdom and spontaneously used his shell phone to contact his old Magical Healer from Belmont. They coordinated a time to meet at the beach, and he began his journey back to the ocean that had once been the scene of his trauma.

The Water Warrior

PART 7

Tony didn't realize until he started his journey back to the ocean just how distant he felt from the dolphins and how he wished fervently to be reunited with them. He was filled with determination to find the Water Kingdom and swim with the dolphins again.

Eventually, he was walking through the rocky areas of Belmont and knew he was close to the ocean. He was happy to be so close to his goal, but an intense fire suddenly blazed in front of him. A malicious laugh from a firebender woman rang out as she began throwing fireballs to block Tony from entering the beach. Tony was stunned and questioned why she was stopping him. She retorted that due to Tony's visibly unmasculine water magic and his superhero shirt, he was not allowed access. Just as he attempted to reason with her, three painfully loud gunshots created an additional threat to Tony. A man with a gun walked over and mocked him. Both the strangers joined together to target Tony by harassing him and knocking him down hard to the ground.

Their cruel behaviors and words made Tony feel very unlike a superhero. Listening to them, he had a vivid flashback to Brian's assault all those years before. He thought of the agony of his dolphin friends fleeing from Brian's sharks and being separated from them for years. As the pair's barrage continued, Tony realized that reasoning with these people wasn't an option, and his safety was in jeopardy. Unlike when he was younger, Tony knew to act swiftly now. However, his water magic: healing spell was his only spell and not something that could actively protect him in this moment.

PART 7

The firebender woman and the gun-toting man stood to block his path to the ocean, mocking him and refusing to allow him entrance. Tony was crouched on the ground, trying to stay calm. He didn't make any sudden movements that might escalate the situation. The strangers' taunting about how they were better than Tony and how he was unworthy made him feel powerless.

Tony was deep in thought. He knew that this assault was pushing him to a darker mental place. Tony refused to give up on reconnecting with his dolphin friends and his childhood fantasy of seeing the Water Kingdom. He reminded himself of his superhero progress over the past several years and knew that his years of training had helped him master his healing spell. During that time, he had aimed to become a superhero who would help other superheroes with their struggles. He knew his true strength was supporting others, not creating chaos or hurt. Tony realized his water magic: healing spell had helped many superheroes on the Superhero Lifeline and recalled that he had never given up on anyone—now he wouldn't give up on himself.

He understood the severity of this situation and wondered if his water magic could help him in this dangerous moment. Filled with renewed confidence, Tony began to stand up, and the piercing water magic began to form a protective wave around him. He knew water was flexible in its application and told himself that he could trust the water for support, protection, and restored strength. Tony also trusted his own resiliency. Sure enough, the water magic began to transform into a new spell as he stood up.

The Water Warrior

Water Magic:
Knight Armor

PART 7

Water magic: knight armor! The water magic shone as it transformed into knight's armor and created a sword with bright-blue gems in Tony's hand. Tony now wore a durable dark-blue suit of armor made of beautiful, luminescent water. On his chest was the semicolon that signified suicide prevention and awareness, representing his hope for universal accessibility to mental health services. Being a knight represented not giving up on himself and reminded him to stand up to ignorant behaviors and hurtful actions.

Tony stood with courage and empowerment. He had pride in his superhero development and felt ready to fight to defend his superhero identities, Superhero Recovery, and the Superhero Lifeline. The firebender and the man with the gun were shocked by his new spell and angry at Tony for not caving into defeat. They mocked Tony's superhero symbol on his chest. Tony emphasized his belief that his superhero symbol would help others and assertively told them to stop their bullying.

They laughed at Tony and launched fireballs and gunshots toward him, but his water armor and boots allowed him to maneuver swiftly across the ground, using water magic to accelerate his speed. Even though the bullets and fire sometimes touched his water armor, the armor protected Tony from all attacks. The cruel pair became outraged and yelled offensive, derogatory terms. No longer listening to them, Tony accelerated his speed toward them and slashed his sword at them. Though they fell down, they did not stop their abuse and claimed they were stronger than him.

Tony responded by stating that true strength is helping other superheroes and that superheroes use their powers to make the world a better place. The firebender and the man with the gun furiously used all their strength to create a massive blow to destroy Tony. The fire grew significantly, and the man sharpened his focus on Tony. Tony refused to lose, knowing the dolphins and the Water Kingdom were on the other side of the rocks. As the fire and gunshots were launched toward him, Tony used water magic: knight armor to slide with his water boots, pierced through their attacks, and used both hands to wedge his sword through them. They were knocked down but still conscious because Tony didn't want to truly hurt them. Leaving them behind, Tony walked toward the ocean.

A Merman With Dolphins

PART 8

After the epic battle, Tony arrived at the beach and saw the same dark ocean he had last swam in as a teenager. There were no dolphins in sight, and Tony felt his nervousness increase. A few moments later, the Magical Healer levitated down with his air magic and greeted Tony with an enthusiastic hello. As they caught up, the Magical Healer was impressed by how Tony had cultivated his water magic to help others and to stand up for himself. As they chatted, Tony mentioned his desire to see the dolphins and find the Water Kingdom. The Magical Healer used his air magic to show Tony striking shades of rainbow colors in the sky, helping him talk through his feelings of seeing the dark water. Tony shared that he felt nervous and anxious entering the ocean again. The Magical Healer used his air magic to help Tony with his breathing to decrease his anxiety.

Tony shared that he strived to have joy in the water like during his youth and also expressed fear of going back in the water because of his suicide attempt. Tony was also worried he wouldn't see the dolphins again and wasn't fully confident that his water magic was powerful enough to accomplish his goals. The Magical Healer supported Tony and emphasized that his magic and motivation were more than enough to reunite with the dolphins and find the Water Kingdom. He suggested that Tony go back into the water and use his water magic: healing spell on himself. He told Tony to consider his younger self as a separate superhero in need of support, just like other superheroes whom Tony had helped. Tony listened carefully and decided to try going in the water. The Magical Healer would remain nearby, should Tony need assistance.

Tony swam through the dark ocean and lay down on his back. Instantly, his anxiety reared up and interjected doubts in Tony's mind: *You're never good enough for anything. Nobody would ever want to love you.* Tony's breathing became ragged, and he began to sweat as his memories of the drowning resurfaced.

Instead of succumbing to the feelings of despair, he remembered his superhero identities, his entire journey, and the suggestion from the Magical Healer. Tony activated his water magic: healing spell to feel comfort in the water. The piercing blue surrounded him, and he began to relax. Tony felt his anxiety and fears slowly drip away from him. The ocean water then gently dipped Tony deeper into the water, and his water magic allowed him to breathe underwater as a new spell morphed around him.

A Merman With Dolphins

PART 8

Water magic: merman king! Because of the water magic: healing spell, the once-dark water transformed into a pure and vibrant turquoise. Tony's magic allowed him to comfortably breathe underwater. His history of butterfly waterbending transformed him into a merman, allowing him to swim like a dolphin. The new trident and crown with a semicolon gem on it made him feel proud of learning a new and powerful water magic spell. There was a sense of ease in having a tail; he moved it freely and twirled around in the water. Tony was once again ecstatic to be underwater!

Swimming in the ocean gave Tony a rush of excitement! When this thrill subsided, he paused in the water. The potent tranquility and fulfillment of moving underwater again made him reflect on his drowning attempt. Back then, he had been in a place where he only thought of dying to end his misery. He remembered his panic and his feelings of self-betrayal at using water to hurt himself but knew that he now had the resources and awareness to never return to that point again. He was aware that other superheroes still struggled with those kinds of thoughts, and theirs may not wash away like his had. He had been completely lost in and uncomfortable with his identity then but now felt satisfied with how far he had come in his self-perception and superhero journey.

Tony combined his new spell with his past butterfly waterbending style to confidently become his authentic self. He never knew that healing himself could be so freeing and meaningful. He would neither deny his pain nor allow negative views from others to influence him. Tony realized that his compassionate self-acceptance had unlocked his new spell. Being a merman felt natural and genuine to Tony's superhero identities. The water had once again become a blissfully safe place.

Out of the blue, three cheerful, disabled dolphins appeared and playfully swam around Tony, greeting him with whistles and clicks of happiness. Proud of his progress, they deemed him worthy of visiting the Water Kingdom and escorted him to the beautiful world he had longed to know. Tony swam with the dolphins lightheartedly, just as he had as a child, and explored the Water Kingdom. The beauty and serenity of the Water Kingdom felt surreal as he took an underwater breath of relief in his emotional journey to reach the Water Kingdom. Tony had achieved his lifelong dream.

Tony: A Forever Learner & Master Of Water

PART 9

Water represents Tony's emotional world and his ability to express himself. When the water reflects Tony's image, he thinks about his relationships, love, self-acceptance, boundaries, and creativity—all the components that make up Tony's flow. He has learned that having an abundant flow has pros and cons. The pros include feelings of joy, innovation, and compassion, while the cons lead to feelings of anxiety, depression, and tears, which are water, after all. Tony's superhero journey encompassed learning how to balance his well-being in a healthy stream of water in his life, not too much water, not too little. Water magic is Tony's control of his emotions, thoughts, and behaviors. The magic symbolizes his development and ability to adapt. Magic has the ability to transform, and it always exists inside each and every one of us when we aim for self-actualization.

What's next for Tony? Tony's superhero journey in and out of the water has only begun. There are many doors still to be opened and countless places still to be explored. Tony is eager to learn more about how he may support others on many levels. He still strives to continue his development as a master of water magic, reflecting each day on how he can use his power to help not only others but also himself.

Tony wants to support other superheroes with their struggles by helping them heal from their pain. Every superhero goes through hardships and has a story waiting to be heard. He wants to work with other superheroes who stand up for social justice and raise awareness on issues impacting mental health. Tony will swim through his flow, always putting humanity and love first. The Water Kingdom is a place where Tony can be himself without judgment or fear. Tony encourages all superheroes to be part of this magical place. His water magic allows others to flourish underwater in the Water Kingdom. He knows that other superheroes may not yet be able to protect themselves; he wants to extend his magic to help anyone who is open to being vulnerable about their superhero struggle. Give him a shout-out on social media or send him your superhero story through email or his website:

https://tonyssuperherostory.com

tony@tonyssuperherostory.com

Thank you very much for following and supporting Tony's superhero story! ☺

Preventing Drowning:
SAFETY IN PODS

Our lives are like ocean waves that persistently come toward us, unpredictable in size and intensity. As humans, we can either dodge the wave or ride the wave and head back to land. Both dodging or riding the waves makes us vulnerable and at risk for harm due to factors we cannot control. A particular issue with avoiding a wave is that another wave follows the prior wave. The second wave that follows could be stronger and potentially trap us, causing us to drown. Perhaps you've felt like Tony before and struggled with your mental health, feeling like you were drowning. Not everyone has been able to cope or survive the treacherous waters of mental health hardships; some have drowned or are currently drowning.

There may be moments in your life when you feel like you are drowning. If you are currently drowning, remember that you are not alone. Please call or text a national suicide and crisis service hotline. Refer to part 4 in *Tony's Superhero Story* to find the shell phone on the Water Reflections illustration for hotline numbers.

If and when you feel safe, take a deep breath and prepare to dive into this activity that Tony has created for you. Think about your life and the obstacles that you've experienced, the hardships you're going through now or that you've already overcome. What has made you feel or makes you feel like you are drowning? Do you feel like you're drowning now or have in the past? How can you prepare for a future drowning?

_____

_____

_____

_____

_____

_____

_____

_____

_____

_____

_____

In times when we feel like we are drowning, we have PODS to support us. PODS are both external and internal factors that help when we experience hardships, crisis, or suicidal ideation. These external and internal factors are protective and are meant to make us feel safe. They help remind us that we have reasons to live so we can stabilize ourselves or support other superheroes.

Tony has created an activity to help you explore and identify your external and internal PODS. The first POD activity will have you identify your external PODS. The external PODS are nouns that give joy to any of your five senses.

Instructions: Choose and write your four nouns that start with letters *P*, *O*, *D*, and *S*. These nouns can name anything except you. Here is Tony's example:

Pizza   P _____

Oceans   O _____

Dolphins   D _____

Superheroes   S _____

Now that you have identified your external PODS, the second activity will guide you through exploring your internal PODS. The internal PODS are adjectives to describe your personality, character, or identity. In the past, Tony has struggled with using encouraging superhero self-talk. Tony has learned though that thinking and speaking superhero self-talk have improved his views on himself and helped him to feel safe.

Instructions: Use the sentence starters below. Add four compassionate or constructive adjectives to your sentences that start with *P*, *O*, *D*, and *S*. When you have completed this, read your internal PODS aloud in this sentence structure:

Here is Tony's example: **Name:** _____

Tony is <u>Passionate.</u>   _____ is _____

Tony is <u>Optimistic.</u>   _____ is _____

Tony is <u>Determined.</u>   _____ is _____

Tony is <u>Sensual.</u>   _____ is _____

TONY'S SUPERHERO SELF-CARE REGIME

Ar

- BREATHING TECHNIQUES
- DANCE
- MUSIC
- PERSPECTIVE SHIFTS

ire

- ARTS AND CRAFTS
- BAKING
- RECONNECT TO YOUR "INNER FIRE"
- TRATAKA

arth

- GROUNDING TECHNIQUES
- HIKING
- NATURE
- STRENGTH TRAINING

Water

- BODIES OF WATER
- DRINKING H2O
- SHOWERS AND BATHS
- SWIMMING

Healing

- EATING MINDFULLY
- FACE MASKS
- REGULAR SELF-CARE
- REST

Magic

- ADVENTURES/ TRAVEL
- ANIMALS
- FRIENDS
- READING

Spirit

- LEARNING
- MEDITATION
- STEP INTO THE UNKNOWN
- TALK THERAPY

Create your own Superhero Self-Care Regime by adding three activities for each domain that work best for you. They can be the same as Tony's examples and/or your own original ideas.

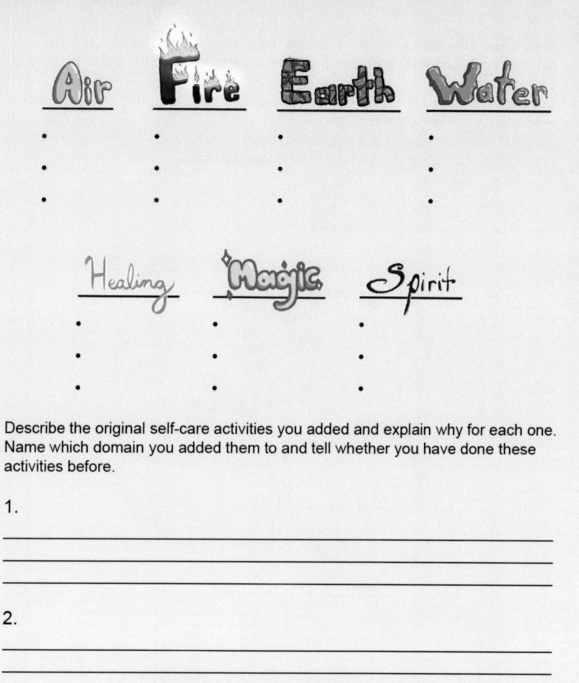

Describe the original self-care activities you added and explain why for each one. Name which domain you added them to and tell whether you have done these activities before.

1.

_____

_____

_____

2.

_____

_____

_____

3.

_____

_____

_____

Superhero Tips for Best
Self-Care Practices

Before and after your self-care activities, take at least one deep breath. This will set your body and your mind to begin your superhero self-care and also resume your day.
Self-care activities are important. Do them daily and at a regular time, and whenever you have a negative emotion.
Do them alone or with others; whatever works best for you!
Do them in a private setting and/or where you can focus.

Anthony "Tony" Santilli, LMFT

References: Becoming a Water Curer Suggestions and Languages

Breathing technique: 4-7-8 technique (Source: Healthline, https://www.healthline.com/)

The following steps should all be carried out in the cycle of one breath:
1. First, let your lips part. Make a whooshing sound, exhaling completely through your mouth.
2. Next, close your lips, inhaling silently through your nose as you count to four in your head.
3. Then for seven seconds, hold your breath.
4. Make another whooshing exhale from your mouth for eight seconds.

Perspective shift: "When we are no longer able to change a situation, we are challenged to change ourselves" (Viktor Frankl).

We can reframe our thoughts. Examples: Instead of dwelling on thoughts such as, *It's all my fault* or *Nobody likes me*, we can choose to think, *There are some things that I cannot control and I am doing the best I can* and *I feel misunderstood, and I'm worthy of good things*.

Arts and crafts. My favorite projects include glitter jars, melting crayons, painting, Perler beads, and photography. Caution: some of these projects are messy. Be prepared!

Reconnect to your "inner fire". "Trust yourself. Create the kind of self that you will be happy to live with all your life. Make the most of yourself by fanning the tiny, inner sparks of possibility into flames of achievement" (Golda Meir).

Identify your passions and motivations, and make a plan to engage in them! Examples: What are things that make you smile? Who do you feel your best with? What makes you feel confident? What do you like to learn about? Where do you go to feel peaceful?

Trataka. A candle-gazing activity. Do not try alone. Attempt only when a guardian or person over eighteen years old is present. This can also be done by gazing at a dot on the wall, the tip of your nose, or a star in the sky (https://3rdritual.com/spotlight/trataka/).

Grounding technique. 5, 4, 3, 2, 1, and hand-on-heart techniques (Source: University of Rochester Medical Center by Melissa Nunes-Harwitt, LMSW, and Sara Smith, BSW).

Eating mindfully. Eat slowly in a peaceful setting, and engage your senses by noticing smells, colors, textures, sound, and flavors. Be aware how food affects your body and emotions and appreciate your food.

Step into the unknown. "In any given moment, we have two options: to step forward into growth or step back into safety" (Abraham Maslow).

Get out of your comfort zone! Examples: Try a new hobby or skill, such as cooking or doing puzzles. Pay a genuine compliment to somebody you don't know. Taste a new food. Stand up for yourself when you need to (e.g., "I have an idea too.")

Elemental Hero Academy Languages
Himali Hawa (Mount Air)—Nepali, Tony taught English in Nepal for three months.
La Isla del Fuego (Fire Island)—Spanish, Tony learned Spanish in Argentina for five months.
Provincia della Terra (Earth Province)—Italian, Tony traveled to Italy to meet some distant family members.
The Dam Falls (Waterfalls)—English, the name is inspired by the animal beavers, which is one of Tony's favorite animals. The beaver represents his travels to Canada and his studies at Oregon State University.

Tony's SUPERHERO Quiz

Hey there, superheroes! I enjoy a good challenge, and I invite you to participate in Tony's Superhero Quiz. This activity is for the superheroes who love solving mysteries and are motivated to answer correctly. There are ten quiz questions about *Tony's Superhero Story*. Best of luck to you!

1.   Which animal taught Tony waterbending?

   A. Dolphins (butterfly)
   B. Otters (backstroke)
   C. Frogs (breaststroke)
   D. Sharks (freestyle)

2.   Which water magic spell does Tony learn first?

   A. Merman king
   B. Knight armor
   C. Healing
   D. Butterfly waterbending

3.   Which part of this superhero story do you speculate was the most emotional for Tony to write?

   A. Changes in the Current
   B. Drowning
   C. Water Reflections
   D. A Merman with Dolphins

4.   What do the rainbow-colored plants in "A Merman with Dolphins" represent?

   A. They represent the beauty of the Water Kingdom.
   B. They represent Tony's denial of his pain and the blissfulness of the water for him.
   C. They represent Tony's favorite colors.
   D. They represent Tony's embrace of his vulnerabilities as part of his identity.

5.   What are the effects of bullying that Tony suffered?

A. Low self-esteem and wanting to fight back
B. He developed water magic and became a superhero
C. Humiliation and emasculation
D. Numbness and shame

6.   Which of these are best represented in the illustration of the firebender woman and the man with the gun?

A. Homophobia and bullying
B. Power and persuasion
C. Violence and turmoil
D. Strength and courage

7.   Compare and contrast the thirteen titles written in black and white. What is the common theme among the titles in black?

A. The titles in black represent Tony's desire to talk to the Magical Healer.
B. The titles in black represent Tony's positive experiences with water.
C. The titles in black represent Tony's confusion about his identity.
D. The titles in black represent Tony's early struggles.

8.   Which of the following does water magic not control?

A. Emotions
B. Behaviors
C. Thoughts
D. Pride

9.   What does the image of the semicolon signify in *Tony's Superhero Story*?

A. Spirit of hope and adventure
B. Pride in Tony's identity
C. Suicide prevention and awareness
D. Courage and empowerment

10.   What is the date when the National Suicide and Crisis hotline telephone number will change / was changed?

      A. February 25, 2022
      B. May 8, 2022
      C. July 14, 2022
      D. July 16, 2022

Congratulations on completing Tony's Superhero Quiz! The answers and rationales for the quiz are on the next page. Anyone who participates in the quiz is a motivated superhero and passes! Shout out to the superheroes who get an exceptional score of 7 or higher!

Answers and Rationales

1. A: Tony learned waterbending from dolphins (part 1, second paragraph).
2. C: Healing (part 5, fourth paragraph).
3. B: The most emotional piece for Tony to write was drowning because reliving the memories of his suicide attempt reminded Tony of his darkest moments.
4. D: The rainbow-colored plants represent the colors on the pride flag, which symbolizes an important part of Tony's identity.
5. C: Humiliation and degradation (part 3, first sentence).
6. A: Both the firebender woman and the man with the gun say homophobic comments and bully Tony with their hurtful words and actions (illustration "The Water Warrior").
7. B: The black titles refer to experiences when Tony feels positive about his water superpowers.
8. D: Pride is not Tony's water magic control (part 9, first paragraph).
9. C: The semicolon is the international symbol for suicide prevention and awareness (part 7, first paragraph).
10. D: July 16, 2022, is when the National Suicide and Crisis hotline number will change (shell phone in the "Water Reflections" illustration).

About the AUTHOR

Photographed by John Castle

Anthony "Tony" Santilli was born in Mountain View, California, and raised in Los Gatos, California. He grew up in the Belwood neighborhood where he competed in swimming for the Belwood Dolphins team. As a teenager, Tony became a swim coach for this team and developed a passion for teaching children and adolescents. Tony later studied at Oregon State University. While studying there for his Bachelor of Arts degree in Psychology and a minor in Spanish, he studied abroad in Buenos Aires, Argentina. Later, he was accepted as an intern to teach English in Nepal for an organization called Trek to Teach.

Upon conferral of his degree from Oregon State University in 2015, Tony began to volunteer for the National Suicide and Crisis hotline while becoming a Registered Behavioral Technician to support children and adolescents with Autism. Over the course of the following two years, he pursued and completed his Master of Arts degree in Counseling Psychology at The Wright Institute in Berkeley, California. After graduating in 2018, Tony worked primarily with youth at schools and a clinic where he delved deeper into play therapy. Tony became a licensed Marriage and Family Therapist in May 2021.

Tony is vocal about the social injustices experienced by marginalized communities and works toward further developing himself as an antiracist and an intersectional feminist. He is a proud member of the LGBTQIA+ community. Tony strives to normalize discussions about mental health and to secure accessible mental health services for everyone. He models this among family and friends, through social media and on psychotherapy sites, by advocating for equality, holistic well-being, empathy, and compassion.

Printed in the United States
by Baker & Taylor Publisher Services